Conscious Love

The gratitude journal that helps you put others first

Lynn Sheets

Edited by: Ameesha Green
Cover design by: Niall Burgess
Proofread by: Gemma Rowlands
Typeset by: Niall Burgess

Conscious Love, Lynn Sheets
ISBN: 979-8-9853387-4-4

For You and those dedicated to loving change

Welcome

Journals are often used to emote and release, to reflect and understand, to process and purge. Most gratitude journals are used to express feelings of gratitude. Unlike other journals, this journal is about making a concerted and conscious effort to not just express feelings of gratitude but also to *act on them*. With this journal, you can harness gratitude to be more loving, and with conscious practice, you can make love a "hardwired" habit.

Conscious love is *empowered love*. When we understand how we impact others and consciously decide how we want to impact others, each of us is empowered. We are empowered to be our best selves by giving our best to others through acts of love, which are often rooted in gratitude. Put simply, we are more empowered to live by the Golden Rule if we keep a grateful mindset and think about how we want to impact others.

That said, this journal is more than just reflecting and appreciating; it is about acting with loving gratitude. It still includes critical elements focused on one's self, namely gratitude and self-affirmation prompts, because you cannot love fully if you do not love yourself first, and we can all use reminders and encouragement. However, this journal shifts the emphasis away from yourself—what you have—to how you can better the lives of others (and yourself by extension)—what you offer.

We often do the best we can with the tools we have, but we can always expand upon and improve those tools. Self-esteem is foundational in your toolkit and a reputable resource is the book *Self-Esteem* by Matthew McKay, PhD, and Patrick Fanning. When you have a secure sense of self, it can be easier to find happiness and contentment. If you're looking for a resource on finding contentment through purpose and self-fulfillment, also consider my book *The Passion Project*.

This journal, *Conscious Love*, builds upon self-fulfillment. It extends beyond what fulfills you personally and emphasizes thinking beyond oneself. Conscious love is about cultivating happiness in others—widening the lens of self-fulfillment to take others into account and truly achieve our greater potential.

The journal prompts you will find here are based on the premise "give, get, be." The more you give through your actions, the more you get in return, and the more you become by doing. What you do regularly becomes a habit. The more love you express, the more love you receive and the more loving you become—and the more loving the world becomes.

This journal can be dedicated to one person or any number of people in your life, and it contains three parts:

Part 1 focuses on who you love and what you want for their wellbeing.

Part 2 focuses on empathy-building and short exercises to love consciously by enacting gratitude.

These exercises can be repeated at any time you need them.

Part 3 is the main body of the journal and it includes daily prompts to action love through gratitude for 60 days as it takes approximately 2 months to build a new habit. In these main prompts, you will chart your own course each day to "hardwire" loving gratitude.

Enjoy the love that your action creates... for both yourself and those around you!

Part 1

My Love

My Love

Who do I love? Who do I want to dedicate this journal to?
I love:

What do I want for them (not thinking about myself)?
I want:

What positive attributes do I consistently bring into the relationship?
I am:

-
-
-

What additional positive attributes do I want to bring into the relationship?
I want to be more:

-
-
-

My Core Tenets

What do I promise to provide in the relationship?
I will provide:

-
-
-

What can I resolve or let go of to better live my core tenets?
I will let go of:

-
-
-

Part 2

Practice

Empathy Exercise

To love is to be vulnerable. Love often means protecting another person more than yourself when they need you. Opening your heart and mind to experience and feel from another's perspective brings your understanding and your relationships to an entirely new level.

Practice: When someone is upset, step out of your body and into theirs and reflect. If and when appropriate, have a conversation with the person to actively listen and understand their perspective.

What did they experience?

What did they feel?

What did they need?

Recall what led up to the events—what happened in the minutes, days, or even years prior? Could a bigger pattern be at play?

How did the timing of your interaction impact the events that unfolded?

What role did you play?

Enacting Daily Gratitude Exercises

You before I

Instead of opening a conversation with, "I...," see how the dynamic changes when you focus on someone else from the start, using a "you-focused" statement, like "You..."

Practice: What "you-focused" statement will you open a conversation with today?

I am responsible for my actions

Just because we weren't directly taught something doesn't mean that we can't figure it out. We can cultivate greater awareness and hold ourselves accountable for the things we can pick up through our life experiences.

Practice: What lessons have you picked up that were not directly modeled or taught? How will you apply what you learned?

I will...

People are individuals

Another person is not an extension of you but an extension of how you treat them.

Practice: How will you impact others positively today?

I will...

Every action has a reaction

Not only does every action have a reaction, every action also influences and feeds chains of reactions. Is there a pattern of behavior you want to change? Pinpoint your specific actions (not personality traits) that fuel an undesirable pattern.

Practice: What will you do to break a pattern?

I will...

Own your reactions

What is your usual mood? Why?

Practice: What will you do to improve how you feel or how you choose to react?

I will...

Impact others as you want to be impacted

We are the sum of our actions, and together, our actions add up.

Practice: If there were millions of you right now in this moment, what would you tell yourselves to do?

I will...

Awareness leads to realization; proactiveness leads to change

Think of a recent interaction that could have gone smoother, and now imagine you got a do-over.

Practice: What will you do differently next time?

I will...

Part 3

Loving Gratitude

Each daily prompt in this part serves a specific purpose.

The first prompt is to acknowledge your love and appreciation.
Be as specific as possible here and try to list more than one thing or person to be thankful for each day.

The second prompt is for intention-setting.
Using the "I am" statement, what qualities encompass who you aspire to be?

These intentions are powerful statements. Intentions are your North Star. Clear intentions help you see a way from the goals you have to the future you envision (that is, who you aspire to be).

The third prompt is for enacting conscious love.
Using the "Today, I will" statement, set your goals. How will you act on your intentions today?

What will you do for others (or for yourself to enable you to better show your love for others)?

These statements can revolve around one theme that you want to focus on, or multiple, but they should be written as specific actions. Write these statements so that you can hold yourself accountable; be detailed enough so you will clearly know whether or not you are doing what you said you would do.

Without purposely trying, you may notice that your "I am" and "I will" statements gravitate towards a small number of central themes over time. Eventually, you may find that some of your statements vary only slightly each day. This familiarity can be a sign of you honing specific qualities that you deem important and wish to embody.

Take advantage of these refinements and similarities as they show up. Repeated practice and purposeful sharpening of a quality will make it a conscious habit, a loving habit that will empower you.

The fourth self-affirmation prompt is to show yourself compassion and support. List at least three top-of-mind self-affirmations that support your "I am" and "I will" statements. Turn to these throughout your day to re-center and remind yourself that you can be who you strive to be.

Finally, the reflection pages are for you to use any time throughout your day. They include prompts to reflect on the day, but allow yourself flexibility. Use the space to reflect, emote, draw, or do what you feel to be the person you want to be for yourself and others.

With that, it's time to get started...

Your journey starts here...

Date: _____

I am grateful for...

....
....
....

I am...

....
....
....
....

Today, I will...

....
....
....
....

My self-affirmations...

....
....
....
....
....

Reflection:

What went well?

What might I try to do tomorrow?

Date: _____

I am grateful for...

I am...

Today, I will...

My self-affirmations...

Reflection:

What went well?

What might I try to do tomorrow?

Date: _____

I am grateful for...

I am...

Today, I will...

My self-affirmations...

Reflection:

What went well?

What might I try to do tomorrow?

Date: _____

I am grateful for...

....

....

....

I am...

....

....

....

Today, I will...

....

....

....

My self-affirmations...

....

....

....

....

Reflection:

What went well?

What might I try to do tomorrow?

Date:

I am grateful for...

I am...

Today, I will...

My self-affirmations...

Reflection:

What went well?

What might I try to do tomorrow?

Date: _____

I am grateful for...

_____

_____

_____

I am...

_____

_____

_____

Today, I will...

_____

_____

_____

My self-affirmations...

_____

_____

_____

Reflection:

What went well?

What might I try to do tomorrow?

Date: _____

I am grateful for...

I am...

Today, I will...

My self-affirmations...

Reflection:

What went well?

What might I try to do tomorrow?

Date: _____

I am grateful for...

I am...

Today, I will...

My self-affirmations...

Reflection:

What went well?

What might I try to do tomorrow?

Date: _____

I am grateful for...

I am...

Today, I will...

My self-affirmations...

Reflection:

What went well?

What might I try to do tomorrow?

Date: _____

I am grateful for...

....

....

....

I am...

....

....

....

Today, I will...

....

....

....

My self-affirmations...

....

....

....

....

....

Reflection:

What went well?

What might I try to do tomorrow?

Date: _____

I am grateful for...

I am...

Today, I will...

My self-affirmations...

Reflection:

What went well?

What might I try to do tomorrow?

Date: _____

I am grateful for...

I am...

Today, I will...

My self-affirmations...

Reflection:

What went well?

What might I try to do tomorrow?

Date: _____

I am grateful for...

....
....
....

I am...

....
....
....

Today, I will...

....
....
....

My self-affirmations...

....
....
....
....
....

Reflection:

What went well?

What might I try to do tomorrow?

Date: _____

I am grateful for...

_____
_____
_____

I am...

_____
_____
_____

Today, I will...

_____
_____
_____

My self-affirmations...

_____
_____
_____

Reflection:

What went well?

What might I try to do tomorrow?

Date: _____

I am grateful for...

....

....

....

I am...

....

....

....

Today, I will...

....

....

....

My self-affirmations...

....

....

....

....

Reflection:

What went well?

What might I try to do tomorrow?

Date: _____

I am grateful for...

....

....

....

I am...

....

....

....

....

Today, I will...

....

....

....

My self-affirmations...

....

....

....

....

Reflection:

What went well?

What might I try to do tomorrow?

Date: _____

I am grateful for...

I am...

Today, I will...

My self-affirmations...

Reflection:

What went well?

What might I try to do tomorrow?

Date: _____

I am grateful for...

I am...

Today, I will...

My self-affirmations...

Reflection:

What went well?

What might I try to do tomorrow?

Date: _____

I am grateful for...

....

....

....

I am...

....

....

....

Today, I will...

....

....

....

My self-affirmations...

....

....

....

....

Reflection:

What went well?

What might I try to do tomorrow?

Date:

I am grateful for...

I am...

Today, I will...

My self-affirmations...

Reflection:

What went well?

What might I try to do tomorrow?

Date: _____

I am grateful for...

I am...

Today, I will...

My self-affirmations...

Reflection:

What went well?

What might I try to do tomorrow?

Date: _____

I am grateful for...

....

....

....

I am...

....

....

....

....

Today, I will...

....

....

....

....

My self-affirmations...

....

....

....

....

....

Reflection:

What went well?

What might I try to do tomorrow?

Date: _____

I am grateful for...

I am...

Today, I will...

My self-affirmations...

Reflection:

What went well?

What might I try to do tomorrow?

Date:

I am grateful for...

I am...

Today, I will...

My self-affirmations...

Reflection:

What went well?

What might I try to do tomorrow?

Date: _____

I am grateful for...

....
....
....

I am...

....
....
....

Today, I will...

....
....
....

My self-affirmations...

....
....
....
....
....

Reflection:

What went well?

What might I try to do tomorrow?

Date: _____

I am grateful for...

....
....
....

I am...

....
....
....

Today, I will...

....
....
....

My self-affirmations...

....
....
....

Reflection:

What went well?

What might I try to do tomorrow?

Date: _____

I am grateful for...

....
....
....

I am...

....
....
....

Today, I will...

....
....
....

My self-affirmations...

....
....
....
....

Reflection:

What went well?

What might I try to do tomorrow?

Date: _____

I am grateful for...

....

....

....

I am...

....

....

....

....

Today, I will...

....

....

....

....

My self-affirmations...

....

....

....

....

....

Reflection:

What went well?

What might I try to do tomorrow?

Date:

I am grateful for...

I am...

Today, I will...

My self-affirmations...

Reflection:

What went well?

What might I try to do tomorrow?

Date:

I am grateful for...

I am...

Today, I will...

My self-affirmations...

Reflection:

What went well?

What might I try to do tomorrow?

Date:

I am grateful for...

....

....

....

I am...

....

....

....

Today, I will...

My self-affirmations...

Reflection:

What went well?

What might I try to do tomorrow?

Date: _____

I am grateful for...

....
....
....

I am...

....
....
....

Today, I will...

....
....
....

My self-affirmations...

....
....
....
....

Reflection:

What went well?

What might I try to do tomorrow?

Date:

I am grateful for...

I am...

Today, I will...

My self-affirmations...

Reflection:

What went well?

What might I try to do tomorrow?

Date: _____

I am grateful for...

....
....
....

I am...

....
....
....

Today, I will...

....
....
....

My self-affirmations...

....
....
....
....

Reflection:

What went well?

What might I try to do tomorrow?

Date:_____

I am grateful for...

I am...

Today, I will...

My self-affirmations...

Reflection:

What went well?

What might I try to do tomorrow?

Date:_____

I am grateful for...

I am...

Today, I will...

My self-affirmations...

Reflection:

What went well?

What might I try to do tomorrow?

Date:_____

I am grateful for...

I am...

Today, I will...

My self-affirmations...

Reflection:

What went well?

What might I try to do tomorrow?

Date: _____

I am grateful for...

I am...

Today, I will...

My self-affirmations...

Reflection:

What went well?

What might I try to do tomorrow?

Date:_____

I am grateful for...

I am...

Today, I will...

My self-affirmations...

Reflection:

What went well?

What might I try to do tomorrow?

Date:_____

I am grateful for...

....

....

....

I am...

....

....

....

Today, I will...

....

....

....

My self-affirmations...

....

....

....

....

Reflection:

What went well?

What might I try to do tomorrow?

Date:_____

I am grateful for...

....

....

....

I am...

....

....

....

Today, I will...

....

....

....

My self-affirmations...

....

....

....

....

Reflection:

What went well?

What might I try to do tomorrow?

Date:

I am grateful for...

I am...

Today, I will...

My self-affirmations...

Reflection:

What went well?

What might I try to do tomorrow?

Date:_____

I am grateful for...

....

....

....

I am...

....

....

....

....

Today, I will...

....

....

....

....

My self-affirmations...

....

....

....

....

....

Reflection:

What went well?

What might I try to do tomorrow?

Date:_____

I am grateful for...

I am...

Today, I will...

My self-affirmations...

Reflection:

What went well?

What might I try to do tomorrow?

Date:_____

I am grateful for...

....
....
....

I am...

....
....
....

Today, I will...

....
....
....

My self-affirmations...

....
....
....

Reflection:

What went well?

What might I try to do tomorrow?

Date:

I am grateful for...

I am...

Today, I will...

My self-affirmations...

Reflection:

What went well?

What might I try to do tomorrow?

Date:_____

I am grateful for...

....

....

....

I am...

....

....

....

....

Today, I will...

....

....

....

My self-affirmations...

....

....

....

....

Reflection:

What went well?

What might I try to do tomorrow?

Date:_____

I am grateful for...

I am...

Today, I will...

My self-affirmations...

Reflection:

What went well?

What might I try to do tomorrow?

Date:

I am grateful for...

I am...

Today, I will...

My self-affirmations...

Reflection:

What went well?

What might I try to do tomorrow?

Date:

I am grateful for...

....
....
....

I am...

....
....
....

Today, I will...

....
....
....

My self-affirmations...

....
....
....

Reflection:

What went well?

What might I try to do tomorrow?

Date:

I am grateful for...

I am...

Today, I will...

My self-affirmations...

Reflection:

What went well?

What might I try to do tomorrow?

Date:_____

I am grateful for...

....

....

....

I am...

....

....

....

....

Today, I will...

....

....

....

My self-affirmations...

....

....

....

....

....

Reflection:

What went well?

What might I try to do tomorrow?

Date:

I am grateful for...

I am...

Today, I will...

My self-affirmations...

Reflection:

What went well?

What might I try to do tomorrow?

Date: _____

I am grateful for...

....

....

....

I am...

....

....

....

Today, I will...

....

....

My self-affirmations...

....

....

....

Reflection:

What went well?

What might I try to do tomorrow?

Date: _____

I am grateful for...

....

....

....

I am...

....

....

....

Today, I will...

....

....

....

My self-affirmations...

....

....

....

....

Reflection:

What went well?

What might I try to do tomorrow?

Date:

I am grateful for...

I am...

Today, I will...

My self-affirmations...

Reflection:

What went well?

What might I try to do tomorrow?

Date:

I am grateful for...

I am...

Today, I will...

My self-affirmations...

Reflection:

What went well?

What might I try to do tomorrow?

Date:

I am grateful for...

I am...

Today, I will...

My self-affirmations...

Reflection:

What went well?

What might I try to do tomorrow?

Date:

I am grateful for...

I am...

Today, I will...

My self-affirmations...

Reflection:

What went well?

What might I try to do tomorrow?

Love is a living thing.
It is an extension of
you.

So, actively
love— consciously love.